# A Benjamin Blog
## and his Inquisitive Dog
# Investigation

# Exploring Deserts

Anita Ganeri

Raintree is an imprint of Capstone Global Library Limited, a company incorporated in England and Wales having its registered office at 7 Pilgrim Street, London, EC4V 6LB – Registered company number: 6695582

www.raintreepublishers.co.uk
myorders@raintreepublishers.co.uk

Text © Capstone Global Library Limited 2014
First published in hardback in 2014
The moral rights of the proprietor have been asserted.

Edited by Dan Nunn, Rebecca Rissman, and Helen Cox Cannons
Designed by Joanna Hinton-Malivoire
Original illustrations © Capstone Global Library Ltd
Illustrated by Sernur ISIK
Picture research by Mica Brancic
Originated by Capstone Global Library Ltd
Production by Helen McCreath
Printed and bound in China

ISBN 978 1 406 27106 5
17 16 15 14 13
10 9 8 7 6 5 4 3 2 1

**British Library Cataloguing in Publication Data**
A full catalogue record for this book is available from the British Library.

**Acknowledgements**
We would like to thank the following for permission to reproduce photographs: Alamy p. 26 (© Joerg Boethling); Corbis pp. 10 (© John Carnemolla), 27 (George Steinmetz); FLPA p. 15 (Imagebroker/Michael Weber); Getty Images pp. 17 (Stone/© Paul Chesley), 18 (Universal Images Group/Auscape), Photoshot p. 16 (© NHPA/Alberto Nardi); Shutterstock pp. 4 (© Galyna Andrushko), 6 (© somchaij), 7 (© Yoann Combronde), 9 (© Denis Burdin), 11 (© Tom Grundy), 12 (© Maxim Petrichuk), 13 (© pixy), 14 (© Isabella Pfenninger), 19 (© joyfull), 21 (© angelo Iano), 23 (© Joao Virissimo), 29 top (© nito), 29 bottom (© azhuvalappil); SuperStock pp. 5 (imagebroker.net/Michael Weber), 8 (age footstock), 20 (Robert Harding Picture Library), 22 (Tier und Naturfotografie), 24 (imagebroker.net/Egmont Strigl), 25 (Mauritius/Frank Lukasseck).

Front cover photograph of the Sahara Desert, Algeria, reproduced with permission of Shutterstock (© Pichugin Dmitry).

We would like to thank Michael Bright for his invaluable help in the preparation of this book.

Every effort has been made to contact copyright holders of material reproduced in this book. Any omissions will be rectified in subsequent printings if notice is given to the publisher.

Some words are shown in bold, **like this**. You can find out what they mean by looking in the glossary.

# Contents

# Welcome to the desert!

Hello! My name's Benjamin Blog and this is Barko Polo, my **inquisitive** dog. (He's named after the ancient ace explorer **Marco Polo**.) We have just got back from our latest adventure – exploring **deserts** around the world. We put this book together from some of the blog posts we wrote on the way.

## BARKO'S BLOG-TASTIC DESERT FACTS

Deserts are the driest places on Earth. They can also be baking hot, freezing cold, and windy – lucky I'm one tough dog!

# What a scorcher

Posted by: Ben Blog | 16 April at 10.48 a.m.

Here we are in the Sahara **Desert** in north Africa, and it's seriously hot. This deadly desert can reach a scorching 50 degrees Celsius (122 degrees Fahrenheit) in the daytime, though it's much cooler at night. Phew! Other deserts, like the Gobi in China and Mongolia, are warm in summer but bitterly cold in the winter.

**BARKO'S BLOG-TASTIC DESERT FACTS**

Deserts are as dry as a bone because they hardly get any rain. In parts of the Atacama Desert in Chile, it hasn't rained at all for hundreds of years. Yikes!

# Sand everywhere

Posted by: Ben Blog | 9 May at 12.06 p.m.

The first thing we noticed about the Arabian **Desert** is the sand – it gets everywhere! The particular part of the desert in this photo is called the Rub al-Khali (which means "Empty Quarter"). It's the world's biggest **sand sea** – bigger than the whole of France.

## BARKO'S BLOG-TASTIC DESERT FACTS

In some parts of the desert, the wind piles the sand up into giant heaps, called **dunes**. These dunes are in the Sahara Desert. The tallest dune, Cerro Blanco in Peru, stands at 1,176 metres (3,860 feet) tall. Time for a little digging...

# Stones, rock, and salt

I used to think that all **deserts** were sandy until I saw this place. It is the Sturt Stony Desert in Australia, and it is covered in masses of small, red rocks and stones. In fact, most deserts are rocky or stony, not sandy, and some are even covered in salt.

## BARKO'S BLOG-TASTIC DESERT FACTS

**Playas** are flat, salty **plains** in the desert. They are formed from dried-up **salt lakes**. This one is in the Mojave Desert in south-west United States.

# Caught in a storm

We're exploring the **desert** in Kazakhstan. We got stuck in a sandstorm. It was so fierce we could hardly see a thing. In a sandstorm, the wind races across the ground, whipping up the sand. You can't breathe very well, and the sand stings your skin.

### BARKO'S BLOG-TASTIC DESERT FACTS

Sand gets like a giant piece of sandpaper. It rubs and scrapes the rocks into different shapes, like these massive mushrooms in Utah, USA.

# Getting into a scrape

Posted by: Ben Blog | 7 August at 8.03 a.m.

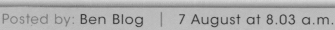

Sand is not the only thing that shapes the **desert**. Check out this photo I took of a deep valley called a **wadi**. When it rains, water rushes along it, carrying along stones and pebbles, which scrape and scour the rocks.

We are here

## BARKO'S BLOG-TASTIC DESERT FACTS

**Mesas** are huge, flat-topped mountains in the desert. They are left behind when the land around them is worn away by the wind and rain. *Mesa* means "table" in Spanish.

# Cool characters

Posted by: Ben Blog | 20 September at 4.43 p.m.

We met some amazing animals on our travels. I managed to take a photo of this little fennec fox in the Sahara. It's a really cool character. Its huge ears aren't just useful for listening out for **gerbils** and other **prey**, they also lose lots of heat to keep the fox's body cool.

**BARKO'S BLOG-TASTIC DESERT FACTS**
A sidewinder snake moves by flipping its
body sideways. That way, it only needs to
touch the hot sand for a few seconds.
Think I'll give it a go...

Another problem **desert** animals have to face is getting enough water. In dry weather, the water-holding frog from Australia shelters in a damp burrow underground. It wraps its body in slime to stop it drying out and stores water in pockets under its skin.

**BARKO'S BLOG-TASTIC DESERT FACTS**

Camels can survive for weeks without eating.
Instead, they live off fat stored in their humps.
They can also go for days without drinking.
But exploring the desert is thirsty work for dogs!

# Blooming desert

Posted by: Ben Blog | 9 October at 1.09 p.m.

Like animals, plants need water to survive. But where do **desert** plants find a drink? I came across this weird-looking plant in the Namib Desert in Namibia. It's called a welwitschia. It uses its long, **frayed** leaves to collect tiny droplets of fog that blow in from the sea.

## BARKO'S BLOG-TASTIC DESERT FACTS

The baobab tree from Madagascar and South Africa has a huge trunk that fills up with water and swells. It's also called the upside-down tree because it looks as if its roots are sticking out of the top.

Remember the Sturt Stony Desert in Australia? I spotted these Sturt's desert peas while we were there. Their seeds lie in the ground for many months until it rains. Then they sprout and bloom very quickly before the desert dries up again.

## BARKO'S BLOG-TASTIC DESERT FACTS

Giant saguaro cacti grow in the United States. They have got different ways of saving water. They store water in their stems, and their sharp spines don't lose as much water as leaves. Ouch!

# Super Sahara

We are back in the Sahara – my favourite desert on Earth. It's also the world's biggest desert. It's larger than the continent of Australia. Amazingly, thousands of years ago, the Sahara was lush and green. These are some ancient cave paintings of an elephant and giraffes that lived there.

## BARKO'S BLOG-TASTIC DESERT FACTS

The Tuareg are **nomads** from the Sahara. They move from place to place in search of water and food. Their long robes keep them cool, and their headdresses keep out dust and sand.

# Danger: desert spread

All over the world, **deserts** are spreading. People are cutting down too many trees for firewood and clearing too much land for farming. This is the Sahel on the edge of the Sahara. It's turning to dust, which is no good for growing crops.

## BARKO'S BLOG-TASTIC DESERT FACTS
The good news is that some deserts are going green! Farmers water the land with giant, spinning sprinklers. This makes round, green fields for growing crops, such as wheat.

# Deadly deserts quiz

If you are planning your own **desert** expedition, you need to be prepared. Find out how much you know about deadly deserts with our quick quiz.

1. Which is the biggest desert?
a) Gobi
b) Sturt Stony
c) Sahara

2. Where is the driest desert?
a) Chile
b) Australia
c) Africa

3. What causes a sandstorm?
a) wind
b) rain
c) cold

4. What is a **mesa**?
a) a pile of sand
b) a flat-topped mountain
c) a groove in the rock

5. How do sidewinders move?
a) by jumping
b) by hopping
c) by flipping sideways

6. What do baobabs store in their trunks?
a) water
b) honey
c) nuts

7. What is this?

8. What is this?

**Answers**

1. c
2. a
3. a
4. b
5. c
6. a
7. cactus spine
8. camel's eye

29

# Glossary

**desert**  place that is extremely dry because it gets very little rain

**dune**  giant heap of sand, piled up by the wind

**frayed**  with torn or ragged edges

**gerbil**  mouse-like desert creature, with long back legs

**inquisitive**  interested in learning about the world

**Marco Polo**  explorer who lived from about 1254 to 1324. He travelled from Italy to China.

**mesa**  huge, flat-topped mountain in the desert

**nomad**  person who moves from place to place to find food and water

**plain**  large, flat stretch of land

**playas**  [say "ply-uhs"] flat, salty plains in the desert

**prey**  animals that are hunted and eaten by other animals

**salt lake**  lake that is filled with salty water

**sand sea**  huge area of sand in a desert

**wadi**  deep valley in the desert that fills with water when it rains

# Find out more

## Books

*100 Things You Should Know about Extreme Earth*, Belinda Gallagher (Miles Kelly, 2009)

*Deserts* (Discover Science), Nicola Davies (Kingfisher, 2012)

*Harsh Habitats* (Extreme Nature), Anita Ganeri (Raintree, 2013)

*The World's Most Amazing Deserts*, Anna Clayborne (Raintree, 2009)

## Websites

**environment.nationalgeographic.com/ environment/habitats**
This National Geographic website covers a range of habitats.

**www.bbc.co.uk/bitesize/ks2/science/living_ things/plant_animal_habitats/read/1**
Learn about habitats on this BBC website.

# Index